Newbridge Discovery Links®

Mars

Mary Kay Carson

Newbridge

A Haights Cross Communications Company

Mars
ISBN: 1-58273-713-4

Program Author: Dr. Brenda Parkes, Literacy Expert
Content Reviewer: Dr. Charles T. Liu, Astrophysicist, Department of Astrophysics,
    American Museum of Natural History, New York, NY
Teacher Reviewer: Sherri Strating, Horace Mann Lab School, Northwest Missouri
    State University, Maryville, MO

Written by Mary Kay Carson
Editorial and Design Assistance by Curriculum Concepts

Newbridge Educational Publishing
11 East 26th Street, New York, NY 10010
www.newbridgeonline.com

Cover Photograph: A view of Mars
Table of Contents Photograph: The Mars Global Surveyor

Photo Credits
Cover: U.S. Geological Survey/SPL/Photo Researchers, Inc.; Contents page: NASA; pages 4–5:
(background) NASA, (inset) U.S. Geological Survey/SPL/Photo Researchers, Inc.; page 5: NASA;
page 6: CORBIS; page 7: U.S. Geological Survey/SPL/Photo Researchers, Inc.; page 8: NASA; page 9:
(left and right) NASA; pages 10–11: (bottom) NASA/SPL/Photo Researchers, Inc.; page 11: (top left)
U.S. Geological Survey/SPL/Photo Researchers, Inc., (top right) NASA; page 12: (top) NASA, (bottom)
NASA/JPL; page 13: (top and bottom) NASA; page 14: JPL/NASA; page 15: NASA; page 16: NASA/
SPL/Photo Researchers, Inc.; pages 17–18: NASA; page 19: NASA/JSC; pages 20–21: NASA; page 22:
Michael Milstein; pages 22–23: Kennan Ward/CORBIS; pages 24–25: Joe Sohm/Photo Researchers, Inc.;
page 26: (top and bottom) NASA; page 27: NASA; page 28: AFP/CORBIS; page 30: Detlev Van Ravenwaay/
SPL/Photo Researchers, Inc.

Illustrations on pages 6 and 7 by Steve Stankiewicz

10 9 8 7 6 5 4

Table of Contents

Meet Mars

Mars is a planet in our solar system that is near Earth. But even though it's our planetary neighbor, no human being has yet paid Mars a visit. If you did, you would see a strange world.

Imagine you are standing on Mars. The sky above is not blue; it is red. All around you the ground is dry and covered with rocks and red dust. The sun looks a bit smaller because on Mars you are farther away from the sun. The planet is silent, except for the wind. There are no plants and no animals to see. There are no signs of life. But there is still a lot to look at.

Our solar system is made up of planets and many smaller bodies that revolve around a star we call the sun. Earth is the third planet from the sun and Mars is the fourth.

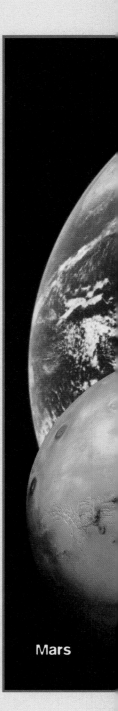

Mars

Earth

Sun

Mercury Venus Earth Mars Jupiter Saturn Uranus Neptune Pluto

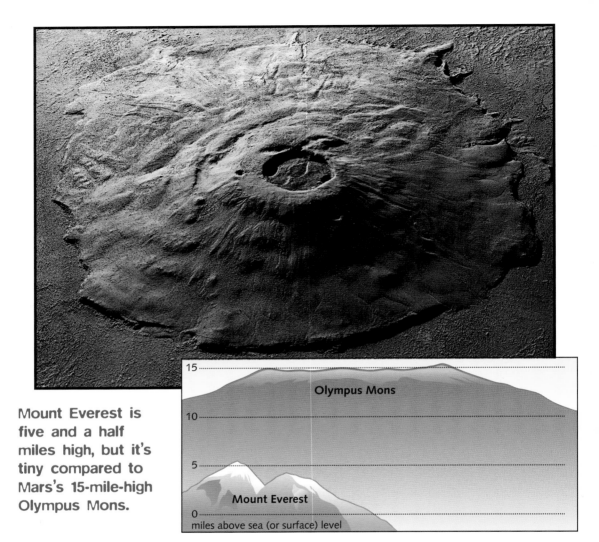

Mount Everest is five and a half miles high, but it's tiny compared to Mars's 15-mile-high Olympus Mons.

Olympus Mons

Mount Everest

15

10

5

0

miles above sea (or surface) level

Monster Landforms

One of the most amazing sights on Mars is a huge volcano. It is so big that if it were on Earth, it would cover the entire states of Ohio, Illinois, and Kentucky combined. Called Olympus Mons, it is the solar system's largest known volcano. The state of Rhode Island would fit in the **crater**, or mouth, of this giant volcano.

You can see other kinds of craters everywhere on Mars, both big and small. They were formed within minutes, as chunks of rock called **meteorites** smashed against the planet's surface.

Mars also has incredibly deep canyons, the deepest found on any of the planets in our solar system. One canyon, called Valles Marineris, is so long that it would stretch across all North America, from New York City to Los Angeles, California. Earth's Grand Canyon is tiny in comparison.

If you stood on one side of the Valles Marineris canyon, and a friend stood on the other side, you wouldn't be able to see or hear each other, because you would be 150 miles apart!

Valles Marineris

Grand Canyon
18 miles wide

Valles Marineris
150 miles wide

0
1
2
3
4
miles below ground level

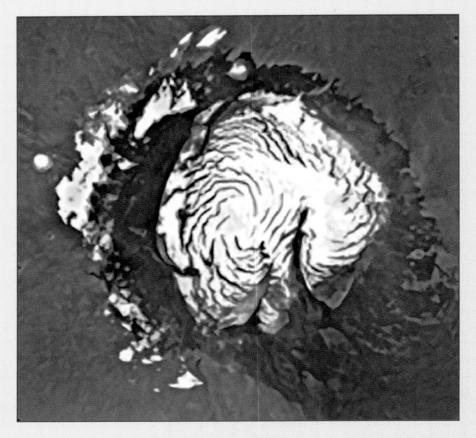

The ice caps grow during the Martian winters and shrink each summer.

Two Ice Caps and Two Moons

It never rains or snows on Mars, but the planet's north and south poles are covered in ice. The ice is actually frozen carbon dioxide, also known as dry ice.

One of the reasons it's so cold is that over billions of years, much of the planet's **atmosphere** has floated off into space. A planet's atmosphere acts like a kind of blanket, keeping the planet warm and protected from space. With such a thin atmosphere, Mars has become a cold world, with an average temperature of about −81°F!

Gravity on Mars is much weaker than that on our planet. But Mars's gravity is still strong enough to hold not one but two tiny moons in **orbit**. If you could stand on Mars and look into the night sky, you would see its two moons reflecting the sun's light. These moons are called Phobos, the Greek word for "terror," and Deimos, the Greek word for "panic." Deimos is just ten miles in **diameter**, or across, and is one of the smallest moons in the solar system.

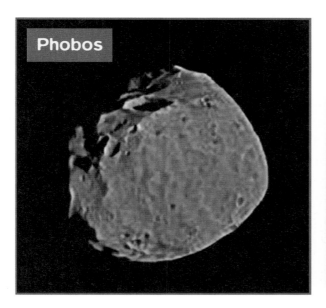

Phobos

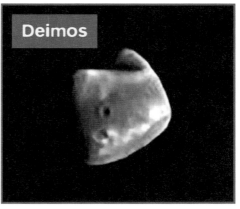

Deimos

Phobos and Deimos look more like potatoes than things that might cause terror and panic. But long, long ago Romans named Mars for their war god. So these scary names describe how it feels to be in orbit around a god of war!

Martian High Jumps and More

There are too many rocks to make Mars a good place for running. The ground is littered with rusty-looking rocks. But if you jumped on Mars, the weaker gravity there might make you a champion. If you can jump three feet high on Earth, you would jump a record-breaking seven feet high on Mars. The lower gravity would change your weight, too. If you weigh 80 pounds on Earth, on Mars you would tip the scale at 30 pounds.

Someone who is 12 in Earth years would be only about six in Martian years! That is because a year on Mars, or the length of time it takes the planet to orbit the sun, is 687 Earth days. That is almost twice as long as a year on Earth.

The surface of Mars is covered with dust and rocks. They look red because they contain a lot of iron oxide, also known as rust. In this photo you can also see a robot from Earth. You'll read more about it on pages 14 and 15.

A day on Earth is 24 hours, which is how long it takes Earth to turn or rotate once on its axis. The Martian day is only half an hour longer than our day! By looking at this chart, what other ways can you find in which Earth and Mars are alike and different?

Mars/Earth Comparisons

	MARS	EARTH
Average Distance from Sun	142 million miles	93 million miles
Diameter	4,220 miles	7,926 miles
Length of Year	687 Earth days	365.25 days
Temperature	Average −81°F	Average 57°F
Atmosphere	mostly carbon dioxide, some water vapor	nitrogen, oxygen, argon, other gases, and lots of water vapor
Number of Moons	2	1
Seasons	4 (but they last almost twice as long)	4

Touchdown!

How do we know so much about Mars? Modern telescopes and space missions have brought us a close-up view of Mars and made possible the "tour" you just took of the planet. In the 1960s, **NASA** launched the first space vehicle that sent information about Mars back to Earth. It was called *Mariner 4*, and it sent back pictures showing many craters, no oceans or lakes, and no cities.

Later, *Mariner 9* orbited Mars. As it traveled around the planet, *Mariner 9* sent back detailed pictures. One goal of the *Mariner 9* mission was to help identify a good spot for the first Mars landing. In 1976, scientists used what they had learned to land two vehicles on Mars. At last it was touchdown! Would the mission find signs of life?

Mariner 9 **photographed many volcanoes and craters on the planet's surface.**

The *Viking* landers had built-in science labs. They scooped up samples of dirt and analyzed them.

Two orbiters searched the planet from above, as a pair of landers studied the soil and climate on the surface. Each lander had television cameras set up to identify anything that might walk over to check out the strange new visitors. The landers also had instruments to analyze the gases and minerals found on Mars. They searched for tiny **microbes**, life-forms too small to be seen without special instruments. But the *Viking* mission did not find any signs of life. Still, scientists were determined to find more ways to study the planet and look for more clues.

Little Rover

On July 4, 1997, the spacecraft *Pathfinder* touched down on the rusty red soil. There were no scientists on board, but when its doors opened, a little rover the size of a microwave oven came out. The rover was called *Sojourner*. *Sojourner* inched along slowly, showing scientists and engineers back on Earth what it's like to move about the surface of Mars. They learned that dust storms can block out the sun, making solar power unpredictable.

Sojourner was a totally new kind of robot. It was actually controlled by a computer operated by scientists all the way back on Earth. You can see the rover's tracks in the photo. The tracks pointed out by an arrow show that *Sojourner* rotated around to take in a full view of its surroundings.

The rover could not bring rocks back to Earth, but it found and analyzed rocks by taking close-up pictures and analyzing the gases and minerals found in them. The scientists back on Earth gave the rocks fun names such as Yogi Bear, Prince Charming, Moe, and Barnacle Bill. From these rocks they learned that Mars was once probably a warmer and wetter place.

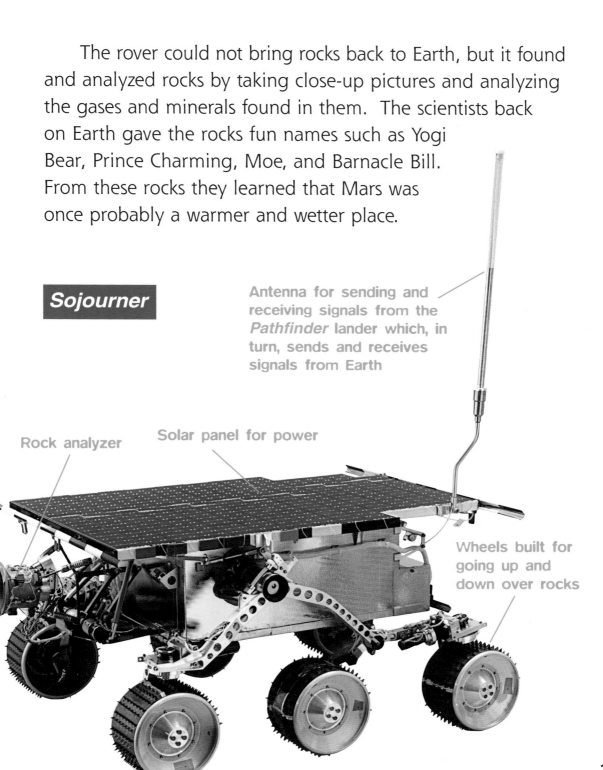

Sojourner

Antenna for sending and receiving signals from the *Pathfinder* lander which, in turn, sends and receives signals from Earth

Rock analyzer

Solar panel for power

Wheels built for going up and down over rocks

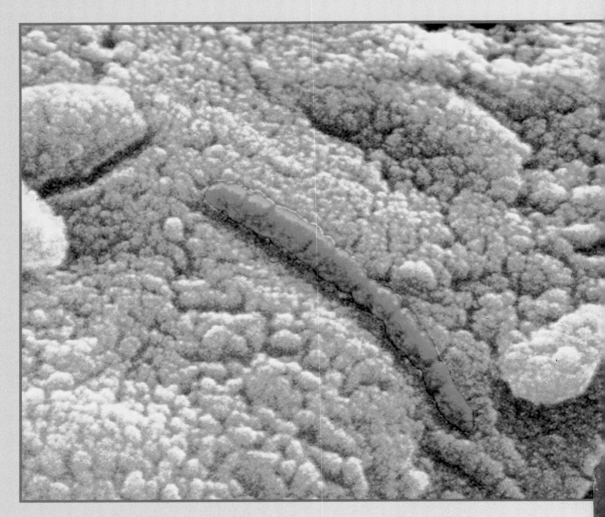

This magnified view shows what some believe is a fossil, 3.6 billion years old, of something that once lived on Mars.

Blast from the Past

This dull-looking piece of gray rock, the size of a large potato, is one of the rarest rocks ever found on Earth, because it is believed to have come from Mars. Scientists think they have found more than a dozen pieces of Mars on Earth. This four-and-a-quarter pound rock was treated as top secret for more than a year, as scientists carefully studied its structure and the materials it is made of. When the scientists announced their findings, a great debate began, one that has lasted to this day. Does this rock contain **fossils** of a life-form smaller than any on Earth? Does it prove that there was once life on Mars?

This painting shows how Meteorite ALH84001 might have started its journey to Earth millions of years ago when it was blasted off Mars.

Stories in the Rock

The rock was first discovered in Antarctica in 1984. It was named ALH84001, which stood for the location where it was found (Allan Hills), the year it was found (1984), and a number (001). But where it came from and what it might contain took years to learn. Scientists found that it was a meteorite, a rock from space, that fell to Earth about 13,000 years ago.

They tested the rock for gases and found that it contained the same gases that space probes had found in rocks on Mars. That's when the excitement, and the search for signs of life, began. Then scientists looked at slices of the Martian rock under powerful microscopes, and found tiny tube-shaped things less than one-hundredth of the width of a human hair (as shown on page 16). Some experts think they look like fossil **bacteria** from Mars.

If they are fossil bacteria, and life did exist on Mars, what happened to it? Is there still life on Mars, or did the planet change?

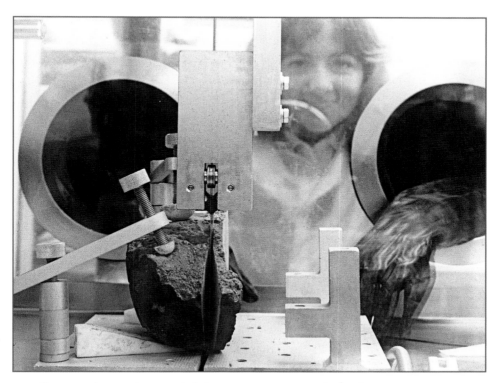

Martian rocks get special treatment at NASA's Johnson Space Center in Houston, Texas.

A CHANGING PLANET

4 Billion Years Ago   3.8 Billion Years Ago   3.5 Billion Years Ago

Could Life Survive on Mars?

Life as we know it could not survive on the surface of Mars. But what if the planet used to be different? There is some evidence that it was. Spacecraft have been looking at Mars since the early 1960s, and maps have been made from the many pictures that have been sent back to Earth. The maps support a theory that the planet was once covered in water.

Today, much of the dry surface is covered with what looks like the remains of ancient lake beds and channels that could have been cut or eroded by rivers. Even though Mars has dry ice at its poles, perhaps it was once a wet world. It could have supported life if it had liquid water.

This diagram, based on studies of the planet's surface, illustrates the theory that water once flowed on the surface of Mars. Areas shown in blue indicate water.

2 Billion Years Ago　　　**1 Billion Years Ago**　　　**NOW**

Ancient Mars was probably very different from the planet we see today. Mars was probably once warmer and wetter, with more air in its atmosphere than it has now. If this is true, then it is possible that life did exist there at one time. Maybe the fossil found in ALH84001 is a record of life from those days. We may never know for sure whether the fossils in the meteorite are really signs of life on Mars. After all, no one knows what a Martian **microbe** might look like, so we have nothing to compare it to. Or do we?

Studying Earth, Understanding Mars

Scientists are looking for similar microbes here on Earth in the warm water of natural **hot springs**, such as those found in Yellowstone National Park. The water in a hot spring is full of minerals and simple life-forms such as bacteria. Billions of years ago, Earth was one giant hot spring, and some scientists hope to prove that ancient Mars was, too. So they are searching Earth's hot springs for microbes, and will compare these to the mysterious tube-shaped things found in the meteorite from Mars.

Learning what the microbes in Earth's hot springs look like will help identify what is in ALH84001. It will also prepare scientists for what they might find someday in the rocks and soil on Mars itself.

Many different kinds of scientists are working together, studying Earth's hot springs. People with training in geology, chemistry, and biology are using what they know about rocks, gases, and life on our planet to make guesses about what Mars may have been like long ago.

A Home on Mars

Perhaps in your lifetime a spaceship carrying astronauts will land on Mars. There are scientists who believe that someday humans may call Mars their home. By forming a colony there, people would be able to study Mars from their own back door.

Experiments on Earth are underway that could make this happen sooner than you might think. The work is being done in places such as Biosphere 2 in Arizona. There, scientists are trying to create a system of plants, gases, and water that can be totally contained within

special housing. Everything needed for life is inside. The plants make oxygen and the soil feeds the plants, so people can breathe the oxygen and eat the plants! If their plan works, it might be possible someday to set up biospheres in harsh places like Mars. It would be like creating little, enclosed Earth-like life, millions of miles away.

It will still be a while before human beings journey to Mars. Those who go to Mars will have to live there for a few years. Just getting there takes six to nine months!

Biosphere 2 is located in the Sonoran Desert in Arizona.

Crater Camp

There is another place where scientists are working toward the day when people will live on Mars. It is called Haughton Crater. It reminds some people of the pictures they have seen of Mars. But this crater is in the arctic region of Canada.

The Canadian Arctic is near Earth's North Pole. It is not as dry and cold as Mars, but it is one of the coldest deserts on Earth. Almost no plants or animals live near the crater. An organization called the Mars Society has worked with

These astronauts are not on the moon or Mars! They are trying out space suits and buggies at Haughton Crater.

An artist shows what a colony on Mars might look like someday. How do the details in this picture compare with the scenes at the rim of Haughton Crater?

NASA to build a special research station at the rim of Haughton Crater. The station is large enough to house six scientists, who try out tools and techniques that may someday be used by astronauts who travel to Mars. Other scientists also camp out near the crater to study its rocks and soil, in order to compare them with findings from Mars.

Odyssey is the first of many missions that are part of NASA's new Mars Exploration Program. NASA plans to send space probes during each Mars launch window, at least until 2015.

The Future

Testing equipment and conditions right here on Earth may help us settle Mars someday. But before that day arrives, more robotic **probes** and orbiters will be sent out to learn even more about Mars.

It's not easy to send missions to Mars! So far, fewer than half the missions launched actually have reached Mars and been able to do their work.

Missions can only be sent about every two years, when Earth and Mars are lined up in a way that makes the trip as short as possible. This is called the Mars **launch window**.

In April 2001, *Odyssey* was launched. It is equipped to analyze the minerals and chemicals that make up the surface of Mars. Scientists are still looking for signs of past or present life. Will *Odyssey* find the proof they hope for? What else will *Odyssey* and future missions discover? And what will happen when a mission finally lands astronauts on Mars?

This is an artist's view of what a future Mars mission might look like.

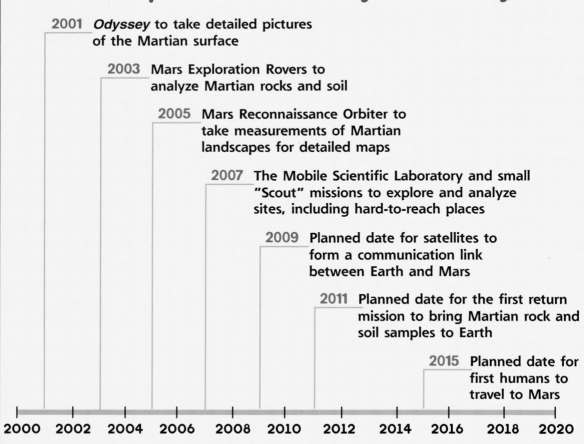

TIME LINE
Mars Exploration in the Early 21st Century

2001 *Odyssey* to take detailed pictures of the Martian surface

2003 Mars Exploration Rovers to analyze Martian rocks and soil

2005 Mars Reconnaissance Orbiter to take measurements of Martian landscapes for detailed maps

2007 The Mobile Scientific Laboratory and small "Scout" missions to explore and analyze sites, including hard-to-reach places

2009 Planned date for satellites to form a communication link between Earth and Mars

2011 Planned date for the first return mission to bring Martian rock and soil samples to Earth

2015 Planned date for first humans to travel to Mars

2000 2002 2004 2006 2008 2010 2012 2014 2016 2018 2020